Date Due			
JAN 30	DEC 6		
MAR 20	MAY 7		
APR 2	OCT 26		
APR 27	APR 19 '76		
APR 28	MAY 16 '77		
MAY 22	MAY 17 1977		
JUL 29	SEP 5 1979		
APR 22			
MAY 14			
NOV 24 '65			
MAR 22			
APR 14			
APR 26			
MAY 24			
MAR 16			
MAY 15			
DEC 19			
APR 30			
MAY 21			
MAY 21			
APR 16			

Demco-293

NORTH STAR
SHINING

NORTH STAR SHINING

A PICTORIAL HISTORY OF
THE AMERICAN NEGRO BY
HILDEGARDE HOYT SWIFT
ILLUSTRATED BY LYND WARD

WILLIAM MORROW & CO., NEW YORK

This book is dedicated to
Chaplain (Captain) Clarence W. Griggs
of the 594th Port Battalion
who was killed in action on Okinawa
April 12th, 1945

NORTH STAR
SHINING

My name was legion,
I came in every slave ship to the Colonies,
In every slave ship.

Mine was the long horror of the middle passage,
The cruel kiss of the whip, the darkness, the burden of chains.
Mine the stench of the hold, the groans of the dying.
Mine the queasy lurch of the ship, the hungry roar of the sea.
Mine the long, long horror and the hope of death,
But still I endured.

I came in every slave ship to the Colonies,
Through the loss of my own freedom
To build a world for the free.

From the beginning of time I was the enslaved one.
    I was the symbol on the coat of arms that Queen Elizabeth
        gave to Hawkins,
    To Hawkins, the bold sea-rover,
    She, the inviolate, the just, the powerful Virgin Queen.
    I was the symbol of his ultimate conquest,
    A black man, bound in chains.

The gold of England was named for me,
    For the coast from which I was taken.
    Oh golden guinea, coined from my anguish,
    Minted out of my suffering,
    Token of man's lust and greed!
Oh infamous token,
    Oh bitter English gold!

I came to the New World empty-handed,
   A despised thing, to be used and broken,
Yet I brought immeasurable gifts.
I brought the gentleness of the Bantu,
   The Dahomian's arrogance and courage.
I brought devotion — and wisdom —
   The knowledge of jungle ways and jungle rhythms,
   Wind-magic and moon-magic,
The knowledge of communion with the mystery men call God.

I stood in the water of the rice fields,
   I bent beneath the sun of the cotton lands,
I mined the ore hidden in the earth,
   I laid the ties of the railroads,
I swung the axes and cleared the forests
   And served in the white man's kitchen.

I built your world, Oh white man, but in the building
   It became mine too.

I brought to the New World the gift of courage.

I was Crispus Attucks — bold, intrepid, daring,
Wild and unpredictable.
In life infamous, I was called
Beggarly wretch, runaway, ne'er-do-well, rapscallion;
Yet in death I became immortal.

I was the first to fall on that memorable night of March
In the year of our Lord seventeen hundred and seventy,
    When the English Redcoats shot at an unarmed people.
Mine was the first blood to stain the snow of Boston.
Though the sober citizens called us "rioters,"
    My death, and the death of the men around me,
    Roused the staid freeholders of Massachusetts,
    Shocked the men of the Colonies into final action,
So that long afterwards, in cold blood, John Adams wrote,
    "On that night the formation of Independence was laid."

My blood was the first to be shed for freedom;
I was Crispus Attucks — wild and unpredictable —
    Who died under a young moon.

I brought to the New World the gift of devotion.

I was Harriet Tubman, who would not stay in bondage.
I followed the devious, uncharted trails to the North,
I followed the light of the North Star,
      I ran away to freedom in 1849.
I was Harriet Tubman who could not stay in freedom,
      While her brothers were enslaved.
"Go down, Moses," back into Egypt,
      Back to the land of the bloodhound and the pateroller,
"Tell old Pharaoh, let my people go!"

Everywhere they waited for my coming,
      Tiny treasures hid against my coming —
I was the lone call of an owl in the darkness,
I was the blurred line of a Spiritual under a slave-cabin window,
I was the last, faint tremor of hope upon the wind.
      I was Harriet Tubman,
      Who "never run my train off the track,
      And never lost a passenger."

14

I brought to the New World the power of self-expression.

I was Frederick Douglass, editor of the *North Star*.
    I was the master of brave, fighting words,
Keen, trenchant words that could not be buried or forgotten,
    Words that grew and grew in men's hearts
    Until they became a forest of marching men.

    "I urge you to fly to arms and smite with death the power
    that would bury the government and your liberty in the same
    hopeless grave. . . "

I was Frederick Douglass,
    There is a statue to me in the public square of Rochester;
        I was the editor of the *North Star*.
        I fought for my people
        With the keen rapier of a word.

I brought to the New World the gift of endurance.

My name was Carney,
I was the standard-bearer for the Fifty-fourth Massachusetts,
In the War between the States.
I carried the colors for Colonel Robert Shaw.

For three nights we had been without sleep,
     For two days without an issue of rations,
But when the word came that we were to support the Union
          fleet and take Fort Wagner,
     We led the attack, boys, we led the attack!

On one side the treacherous, bottomless marsh,
     On the other the sea;
Before us the sweeping line of Rebel fire —
I climbed the walls of Hell that night,
     To plant Old Glory on the very parapet
     Before I fell to a nameless grave.

I was Carney — and I planted the red-blue flower of courage
          at Fort Wagner.

I brought to the New World the gift of fidelity.

I was the Negro who would not leave the plantation;
     How could I run away when there was work to be done?
Even when freedom was offered me, I would not take it.
     Why should I go off with those low-down traipsin' Yankees?
     Why should I leave the plantation I loved?

Early I learned to sing in slavery,
     To dance and cut a caper, and ease the heavy load.
     "Hi, my rinktum! En den dey shake der feet,
     En grease derself wid de good ham meat!"

I was "Old Faithful," who watched at the tomb of Washington;
Come rain or shine, I watched at that tomb,
An' obsequified the white folks who come flockin' to Mt. Vernon.
"Yes, ma'am, yes, sir, the General surely lies here —
Yes, *sir*, I was born on this plantation an' my father before me—
     Yes, ma'am, I'm mighty proud!"

They called me "Old Faithful." Didn't hardly need no other name.

I brought to the New World the gift of communion.

I was the Negro who by many a lonely campfire
    Learned to "steal away to Jesus" on wings of song.
His was the presence standing there beside me,
    Wounded hands and side, and thorn-bent brow.
"Come unto me all ye that labor and are heavy-laden—"
    "Oh Lord, I'm heavy-laden, I'm heavy-laden!"
    "By and by I'm goin' to lay down this heavy load—"
    "And I will give you rest."

He was the Power that saved me from the bloodhounds —
    "Didn't my Lord deliver Daniel, deliver Daniel,
        deliver Daniel?
    Then why not every man?"

Old jungle rhythms half forgot — old atavistic fears —
Out of loneliness, need, and anguish
    Was born the Spiritual,
    A ladder of beauty leading straight to God.
    "A wheel an' a wheel an' a wheel,
    Way up in the middle of the air."

Our name is legion;
　　There are thirteen million of us now.
We are a potent force in America,
　　We are America.

　　I am the man in the ranks,
　　I am a taxi driver,
　　I am a Pullman porter,
　　I am a mailman,
　　I stow freight;
　　I paint ships.
You may not know our names, but we know you,
　　Oh yes, we know all about you!
We do the hard, dull work that needs to be done.
Why not — it's there to be done, isn't it?
It's there to be done.

I'm No. 162,
    Redcap at the Grand Central.
Been here thirty-seven years,
    Feeding the hungry trains —
People, baggage — baggage, people —
    They're gluttons — these trains!

"No, sir, that's not the quickest way to the restaurant.
    I know all the short cuts.
Ought to. I've been here thirty-seven years.
Let me carry that bag, lady; I know it's heavy.
Yes, ma'am, I'll be back for you at one, sharp.
I treat all alike, fair an' square an' honest.
    No, ma'am, I've no time for trips!"

I'm No. 162,
    Redcap at the Grand Central
        For thirty-seven years.

We are the names high on the scroll of honor,
       We have achieved education, fame — and power.
No avenues are closed to us; we have blazed the trails
       for others; we are still blazing them.
We have followed the North Star, Oh yes, we have followed
       the Star!
       We are musicians, writers, teachers,
       Doctors, lawyers, scientists,
       Artists, college presidents,
       Ministers, actors, statesmen.
       Booker T. Washington, James Weldon Johnson,
       George Washington Carver, Paul Robeson,
       Channing Tobias, Shelby Rooks, Walter White,
       William H. Hastie, Louis T. Wright, George Haynes,
       Max Yergan, Mary M. Bethune,
       William Lloyd Imes, Charles S. Johnson,
       Richard Harrison, Roland Hayes,
       Marian Anderson, Dorothy Maynor,
       Joe Louis, W. E. B. DuBois,
       Augusta Savage, Arna Bontemps,
       Richard Wright, Langston Hughes, Countee Cullen.

These — and many others.

I am Roland Hayes,

     Whose songs are known wherever music is loved.

I am Roland Hayes who sang my way around the world.

     I sang to the King and Queen of England,

     In all the capitals of Europe,

     In France and Germany, Italy, Russia — and Spain.

After the first World War, when hate stood against hate,

     And nation against nation,

I sang my German songs to the French, my French to the Germans.

"You will be mobbed," they told me. "Your life is in danger."

I stood up calmly and sang the great songs of the world;

The people gave me thunderous applause.

I proved that Art is a universal language,

     I proved that music transcends the narrow barriers of hate.

I am Roland Hayes,

     Whose songs are known wherever music is loved.

Most of all, I was the fighting man—
      Airman, transport man, Marine —
I was the man behind the tommy gun,
      Behind the hand grenade.

We came from the tenements of Harlem,
      From Georgia farmlands,
      From the classrooms of Fisk, or Talladega, or Hampton—
            or Harvard,
      From the water front of San Francisco.

The "Tan Yanks" came at your call, Oh America,
      We came at your call!

We were in India, Africa, Italy, France,
      At Normandy, Anzio — and Okinawa.
      Oh yes, we died at Okinawa.

This was our War, too, America,
      This was our War, too!

34

I am Robert Brooks who died in the Philippines,
The First War Casualty of the United States Armored Forces.
The parade ground at Fort Knox has been named Brooks Field.

I am Private Henry Williams, Company D, 370th Infantry Regiment.
They gave me the Combat Infantry Badge for "gallantry" near Viareggio,
      And they gave me the Purple Heart.

I am a G. I. from South Carolina,
Sergeant Marcon Johnson, of Company J, the 23rd Infantry,
      the Third Army.
At a ceremony in Czechoslovakia,
I was given the Order of the Soviet Union by a Russian General.

I am Private George Watson, from Alabama.
They gave me the Army's second highest honor
      For going to the rescue of my sinking comrades.

I am First Lieutenant Vernon J. Baker, Rifle Platoon leader of
      the 92nd Infantry.
For "extraordinary heroism in action" they gave me the D.S.C.

I am Captain L. Thomas of Michigan,
Who led a break-through of the Siegfried Line
      With my platoon of tank destroyers.
I was given the D.S.C.

I am Captain Charles B. Hall of Indiana.
I shot down two German planes
      Preparing to strafe our troops on the Anzio beachhead.
Throughout the Italian campaign
      I flew eighty-seven sorties.
They gave me the Distinguished Flying Cross.

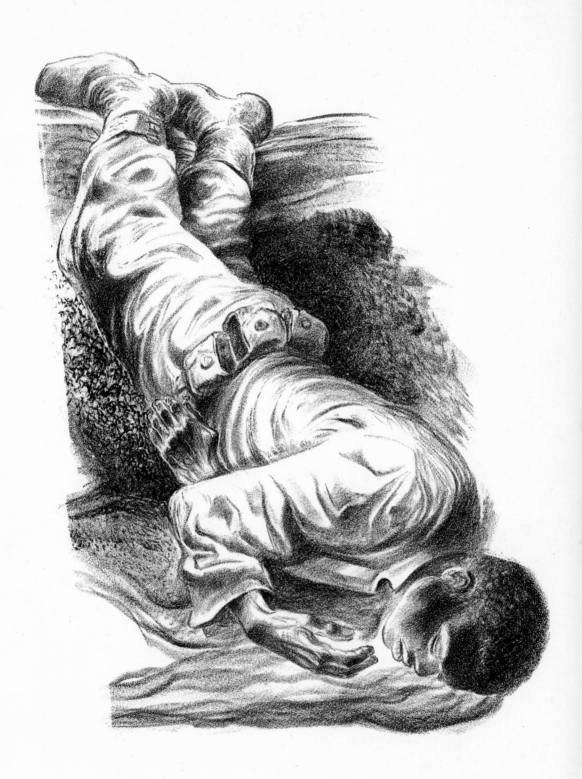

We were these, Oh America,
    And more than these.
We were the hundreds of *unknown*, unhonored heroes
    Who, in the simple line of duty,
    Served the country we loved.

We were the "Tan Yanks."
    This was our War, too.

I am Dorie Miller, mess-boy of the *Arizona*,
       Dorie Miller, who wasn't asleep at Pearl Harbor!
When the Rising Sun shone in infamy from December skies,
       I stood unwavering under its brutal rays.

"Yes, I was just collecting laundry when the alarm for
       General Quarters sounded,
And I headed for my battle station.
No, I'd never shot an antiaircraft gun before,
       But I'd watched others shoot 'em,
So I pulled the trigger and she worked just fine."

I went to my captain on the bridge when he was mortally wounded;
I rescued the wounded, and tended the dying,
       But I went back to that gun.

Admiral Nimitz himself pinned the Cross of Bronze on my breast.
Now I have long since gone to a nameless grave,
       But I'll never be nameless while America stands,
              No, I'll never be nameless.
I am Dorie Miller, mess-boy of the *Arizona*.

Our name was Legion,
  We came in every slave ship to the Colonies,
    In every slave ship,
      Bringing unpredictable gifts.
We brought the agony of the dispossessed,
  The Judas-gold of the slave block,
    The long horror of fratricidal strife,
The bitter, writhing fruit of the lynching tree,
And the clear beauty of a Spiritual rising to the moon.

We were the named,
  And the nameless,
Carney — and Carver, Douglass — and Dorie Miller.
  These, and more than these.

No longer to be shackled and enslaved,
  No longer to be dispossessed and denied,
    We have become a mighty race,
      Dreaming your dreams, Oh America —
  Our genius has become your genius,
    And your pride has become our pride.

I am Clarence Griggs, who died at Okinawa.
    I died for freedom, too.
Oh yes, I knew what freedom meant.
I knew the long, slow struggle up to win an education —
    And hold it —
    I knew.

I was a chaplain, gentle, kindly — keen.
I would have led my people in the paths of peace;
Instead, I served them in the wrack of war.

I died for freedom — for a different world,
Where men forget to hate and stand as brothers,
    Yellow and white and black, together — one.

I died for you — and you — and you —
    Oh do not fail me! Build a world united,
    Out of the shadows
    Turning toward the sun!

The author wishes to express thanks to
Mrs. Clarence W. Griggs for permission to dedicate this book
to her husband; to Miss Gladys McDonald of the *Amsterdam
News* for material on the Negro soldiers, the Tan Yanks
whose names, both the living and the dead, are given in the
text; to the Harris Estate for permission to quote two lines
from "Uncle Remus," used on page 20; to Dr. Channing H.
Tobias, Mr. Arthur W. Hardy and Dr. Charles S. Johnson
for their criticisms; and also to Mrs. Augusta Baker Alexander
for her suggestions, as well as for those of the Interracial
Youth Council. Words put into the mouths of real
persons named in the text are of course the
author's own effort at interpretation.